18th Att Birthday
July 1985
Gift of Hal and Susan Fielding
Santa Fe

Jack Flynn

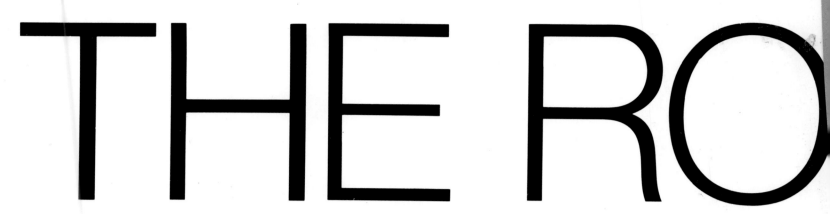

THE RO

Published by Gallery Books
A Division of W H Smith Publishers Inc.
112 Madison Avenue
New York, New York 10016

Produced by
Bison Books Corp.
15 Sherwood Place
Greenwich, CT 06830

ISBN 0-8317-7428-2

Printed in Hong Kong

10 9 8 7 6 5 4 3 2 1

CKIES

TEXT	JEAN CHIARAMONTE MARTIN
DESIGN	MIKE ROSE

GALLERY BOOKS
An imprint of W.H. Smith Publishers Inc.
112 Madison Avenue
New York, New York 10016
A Bison Book

For Mom and Dad

*3/6 A panoramic view of the Grand Teton range,
Grand Teton National Park, Wyoming.*

INTRODUCTION

The Rocky Mountains present over 2000 miles of unequalled natural beauty stretching along the Continental Divide from Santa Fe, New Mexico all the way to the wilderness north of Jasper, on the Alberta/British Columbia border in Canada. Preserved by national parks and forests and by the sheer inaccessibility of much of the terrain, the Rockies comprise one of North America's most pristine wilderness areas. Much of the land still belongs to the abundant wildlife: bison graze in peace in Yellowstone's Lamar and Hayden Valleys, huge grizzlies roam forest and meadow, bald eagles circle far above sparkling rivers in search of fish. Even where man lives in villages tucked away in high remote valleys, mountain goats perch on treeless peaks and mountain lions hunt at night close by. One of the great charms of the Rockies lies in this timeless coexistence between man and nature.

Another attraction is the grand scale on which this whole area has been built. Towering snowcapped mountains yield to valleys filled with colorful wildflowers in spring; steep hillsides flame with golden aspen and larch in autumn; alpine lakes gleam emerald and turquoise beneath a vast blue sky. In Utah, strange rock formations challenge credulity with their ever-changing colors, variety of shapes and gargantuan size. Faced with this stunning plenitude of natural riches, man can only wonder at the unbridled forces which created this earthly paradise.

The Rocky Mountain range can be distinguished from other neighboring chains by the fact that it was born during the Laramide Orogeny, a period of uplift which began some 100 million years ago. As the North and South American tectonic plates began to push away from the Eurasian and African plates, the westward movement brought about a collision with the eastward-moving Pacific plate. The result was the immense buckling we now recognize as the Rocky Mountains. The entire level of the land later rose in a second uplift, so that the base of the Rockies is now about one mile above sea level. The Grand Tetons in Wyoming, rising 7000 feet above Jackson Hole without foothills, are a dramatic testament to the tremendous power of the colliding continental plates.

Other ranges within the Rockies, such as the San Juans in Colorado and the Absarokas in Wyoming, have been shaped by subsequent volcanic activity, while glaciers of the Ice Age have carved a characteristic landscape of U-shaped valleys, moraines (earth and stone deposits), cirques (deep semicircular basins surrounded by steep mountains) and aretes (knife-edge ridges) throughout the Rockies. Glaciers still remain in Glacier National Park,

Montana and in the Canadian Rockies, and thermal activity continues in Yellowstone National Park, Wyoming, where explosive geysers, steaming hot springs and hissing fumaroles (steam vents) are proof of a young land still in a state of violent flux.

People first came to the Rockies as long as 50,000 years ago, perhaps by crossing a land bridge across the Bering Strait which joined Siberia and Alaska. These nomadic hunter-gatherers moved south into the Rockies from Alaska, and remnants of their crude stone tools still occasionally turn up. The Spanish discovered the Rockies in 1540, but explored only the southern region, in New Mexico. Then in 1793 the Canadian explorer Alexander Mackenzie became the first European to cross the continent, and a fur trading company was established at the foot of the Rockies in British Columbia. In the United States, Meriwether Lewis and William Clark were despatched by President Thomas Jefferson to explore the newly-acquired Louisiana Territory, and they discovered the Northwest Passage in 1805. Hardy trappers soon made the Rockies their domain, trading beaver furs with the Indians or selling them to the fur trading companies which sprang up from Canada through Colorado. These mountain men were truly North America's first pioneers.

By the mid-1840s the fur trade was in decline, and pioneers heading for the promise of gold and rich farmlands of the West Coast began to pass through the virgin territory, along the Oregon Trail. The Mormons alone remained to make their home in Utah, irrigating the impossibly dry land and reaping success. Then in 1859 gold was discovered near Central City, in an area called Pikes Peak at the time, and the Colorado Gold Rush was on. Prospectors arrived by the thousands throughout the 1860s, hoping to strike it rich. They gradually moved northward into Idaho and Montana, staking their claims and panning every inch of every creek. In Canada the Fraser River Valley and the Cariboo Valley also drew hordes of prospectors lured by the scent of gold. By the end of the decade the gold boom was over, and the miners, most of them disappointed, drifted away.

Meanwhile the Pony Express and the stagecoach of the Old West were giving way to railroads. In 1869 the first cross-continental railway was completed in the United States; by 1886 Canada had its transcontinental line. The Homestead Acts encouraged people to settle the mountain valleys, and many cattle ranchers came to the area. Unfortunately the Indians suffered greatly during this time. The buffalo were nearly wiped out and the Indians were forced to leave their lands, herded high into the mountains or into arid country were survival was nearly impossible. They rebelled, and bloody wars were fought for many years, ending finally with the Battle of the Little Big Horn in 1876.

Mining became big business when, aided by the arrival of the railroads, lode mining took off in the 1880s. These mines lasted longer and required more manpower than placer mining, and such boom towns as Leadville, Cripple Creek and Silverton, Colorado, grew up around them. Saloons and gambling halls provided recreation for the rough and ready men who came to these towns for work, and a rowdy atmosphere of drinking and brawling prevailed. Sheriffs tried to maintain a semblance of order, but more often a shootout would resolve a dispute. Eventually many of these mines too went dry, or it simply became too expensive to extract the minerals any longer. Abandoned mine shafts and ghost towns attest to the wealth hidden in the mountains, and mining still goes on in locations throughout the Rockies.

In 1872 Yellowstone became the world's first national park, and many more have followed in both the United States and Canada. State and provincial parks as well as national forests also protect great tracts of land from uncontrolled development, so that the Rockies remain much as they were when Jim Bridger first described them over 150 years ago. In the twentieth century, the Rockies have become a favorite vacationland, and those who visit the mountains come not to exploit the land but to carry away only photographs and fond memories.

The Rockies' inhabitants have traditionally been an adventurous breed, and the frontier spirit is still strong in many of the small towns throughout the region. Many people continue to go west, lured by the high tech boom in Colorado or by the sublime beauty of the mountains and the wealth of recreational activities, from fishing to backpacking to ballooning, as well as some of the best skiing in the world.

But perhaps the best way to enjoy the Rockies is simply to walk away from the crowds and into the wilderness a bit. Breathe the intoxicating scent of lupine in a meadow; listen to the rush of a river; watch quietly as a moose and her calf drink at a pond. Allow the mountains to draw you into their harmony and tranquillity for just a little while, and feel yourself a part of nature in the Rocky Mountains.

COLORADO AND NEW MEXICO

Colorado is the roof of the Rockies. In all, the state has 54 peaks over 14,000 feet, proudly referred to as 'Fourteeners' by Coloradans: Mount Elbert is the highest, at 14,433 feet. The highest peaks are in the Sawatch Range in central Colorado, but Fourteeners are also found in the San Juans in the South, and the popular Front Range, which forms a dramatic backdrop to capital city Denver and booming Colorado Springs and Boulder. All this makes for some of the most exciting hiking and skiing in the country.

Just getting around the state by car, bicycle or railroad can be an adventure. The famous Million Dollar Highway between Silverton and Ouray in the western San Juans climbs steeply to 11,018-foot high Red Mountain Pass and falls away just as steeply on the other side. And the Durango and Silverton Narrow Gauge Railroad, relic of the great Denver and Rio Grande Railroad which served mining communities during the Gold Rush, runs for 45 breathtaking miles along the course of El Rio de las Animas Perdidas, The River of Lost Souls.

Denver, the biggest city in the Rockies, began as a chaotic gold rush town and grew up during the energy boom after World War II. The city continues to grow now, with high tech industry turning the Front Range into another Silicon Valley. In the last decade, the Mile High City has had a 30 percent increase in population, and 16 new skyscrapers have gone up. Other population centers include Colorado Springs, with its huge Air Force base, and high tech Boulder, with a youthful, health-oriented character which in many ways epitomizes the new West.

Colorado also has numerous small towns tucked away in the mountains, many of which contain beautiful old Victorian homes. Such gold rush towns as Leadville, Silverton, Central City and Georgetown rely on relics of the past to draw tourists today, while other former mining towns such as Aspen, Telluride and Crested Butte have become popular ski resorts. In the summer, music festivals and sporting events enliven many Colorado towns.

Wilderness areas and national forests throughout the Colorado Rockies offer spectacular scenery and excellent opportunities for outdoor recreation. Rocky Mountain National Park, north of Denver, is a popular destination; Pikes Peak, south of Denver, is a famous landmark from gold rush days; and the Maroon Bells, in the Elk Mountains near Aspen, present one of the most photogenic scenes in all of the Rockies.

National monuments include Dinosaur and Florrisant Fossil Beds, which contain extensive fossil remains; Great Sand Dunes, where vast sand dunes have piled up at the foot of the Sangre De Cristo Mountains; and the precipitous Black Canyon of the Gunnison. In southwestern Colorado, Mesa Verde National Park is the site of a spectacular set of cliff dwellings built into the canyon walls by the mysterious Anasazi Indians.

The southernmost end of the Rockies runs into arid northern New Mexico, where the oldest communities in North America are situated. The Mexican influence is evident in the adobe dwellings of the region, which blend well with the earthy shades of the dry mountains. Artists are drawn to Taos, where the desert light playing on the mountains creates a mystical atmosphere. Santa Fe, the capital of New Mexico, maintains its historic charm with its central plaza, traditional Spanish churches and green secluded courtyards. The red rock Jemez Mountains, a volcanic range, and the Sangre de Cristos, fade into foothills as they approach their southern terminus at Santa Fe.

13 Columbines carpet the Yankee Boy Basin below Mount Sneffels in Colorado's San Juan Mountains.

14/15 Alpine sunflowers face the early morning sun in the Needle Mountains near Ophir Pass in the San Juan range.

16 top A spring skier enjoys the sun on a ski lift high above Telluride.

16 bottom The Steamboat Ski Band is a favorite at the Steamboat Springs Winter Carnival Parade.

17 Colorado Springs, second largest city in the state, is situated below Pikes Peak, once the focus for gold-rushers and now a popular tourist destination.

18 *The thrill of skiing in fresh powder at Aspen, with an awesome view of the Colorado Rockies as a backdrop.*

19 *Dogsledding is clearly the best way to get around in the snow-covered hills near Snowmass.*

20 The rush of whitewater rafting on the Arkansas River appeals to those with a taste for adventure.

21 A different kind of rush comes from hiking in the high country, such as the area surrounding Mount Gilpin, where the altitude and fresh air combine with spectacular scenery.

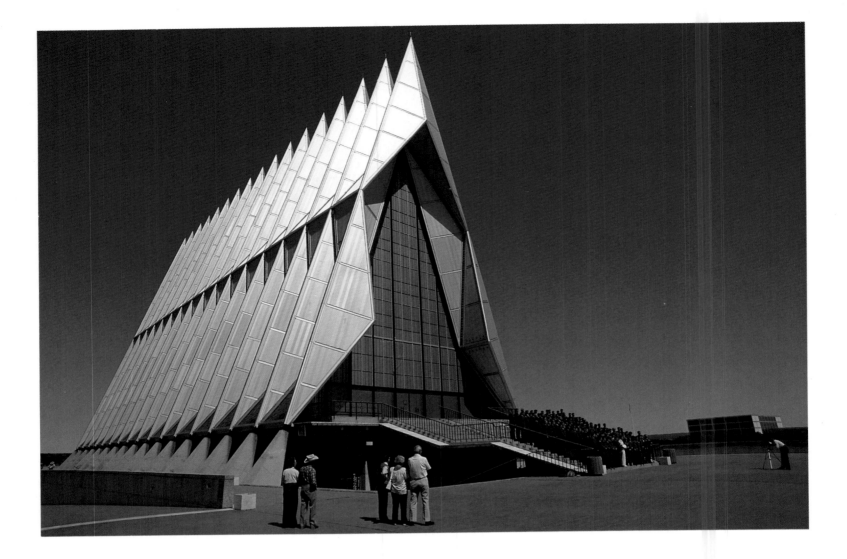

22 A choir sings on the steps of the US Air Force Academy Chapel at Colorado Springs.

23 top Red Rocks Theater, west of Denver, is built into a natural amphitheater of red rock walls that rise 400 feet on two sides, with a superb view of Denver on a third side.

23 bottom The Maxwell House in Georgetown is a gem of Victorian architecture.

24/25 The modern skyscape of the Civic Center in the Mile High City, Denver. Colorado's capital offers the excitement and prosperity of a booming city with easy access to the grand mountains of the Front Range.

26 A scene from another era: The steam-driven Durango and Silverton Narrow Gauge Railroad thunders through breathtaking Cascade Canyon just as it did when it served mining communities at the turn of the century.

27 Window-shopping in Central City's well-preserved historic district, which recalls the glory days of the 'richest square mile on earth.'

28/29 Colorful hot-air balloons are inflated in preparation for a day's sport at Chatfield Reservoir.

30/31 Surrounded by bright yellow aspens, the Maroon Bells in the Elk Mountains are a perfect symbol of the beauty of a Colorado autumn.

32 Mountain lions reside in the Colorado Rockies, but are rarely seen because they are nocturnal.

33 top No animal is better suited to alpine life than the nimble-footed mountain goat. This pair was photographed in the Mount Evans Wilderness.

33 bottom A pronghorn antelope munches on black-eyed susans in open grassland.

34/35 The Cliff Palace at Mesa Verde National Park is perhaps the most impressive cliff dwelling left by the mysterious Anasazi Indians of the Southwest.

35 The twisted bark of a hardy juniper hugs the red rock before reaching skyward.

36/37 The gentle curves of the Taos Mountains in New Mexico are at the southernmost end of the Rockies.

38 An old-timer in Las Vegas, New Mexico stands near a whitewashed adobe wall and vivid blue trimmed door typical of the Mexican architecture in the northern part of the state.

39 The picturesque chapel of San Geronimo de Taos and a traditional adobe dwelling in Taos Pueblo, New Mexico. The town has been continuously occupied by Pueblo Indians since the fourteenth century.

40 A Pueblo boy performs a traditional dance. The Pueblo have tenaciously preserved their cultural heritage.

41 The Indian Market in charming Santa Fe, the capital of New Mexico. Facing the marketplace is the Romanesque Saint Francis Cathedral, built in the 1870s.

UTAH

In 1846, Brigham Young organized the followers of a new faith called Mormonism to migrate west in order to escape religious persecution. Twelve thousand people moved through Iowa toward the land they called Zion, the isolated valley of the Great Salt Lake in Utah. From there they spread out to settle the dry, hostile land successfully and practice their religion freely. Today the Latter-Day Saints maintain their insularity, yet they have made their peace with the modern world to a certain extent and have become one of the country's wealthiest religions.

Salt Lake City is the capital of Utah and of the Mormon religion. At its center is the six-spired, neo-Gothic Latter-Day Saints Temple, crowned by a gold statue of the Angel Moroni. With the arrival of new high tech companies, Salt Lake City has become a truly modern city of opportunity in an attractive setting. The nearby Wasatch Mountains now boast such popular ski resorts as Alta, Snowbird and Park City.

Southeastern Utah is part of the vast Colorado Plateau, a high tableland formed by uplift which began about 65 million years ago. Between 20 and 40 million years ago, volcanic activity formed the Henry, Abajo and La Sal Mountains, while the Colorado River and its tributaries continued to cut through the mesa to form gorges and canyons. Millions of years of erosion caused by wind, rain and frost have sculpted the spectacular pinnacles, arches, domes, hoodoos and bridges which make up the bizarrely beautiful landscape of southern Utah.

North of Moab, the largest city in southern Utah, is Arches National Park, which has the most impressive concentration of natural red sandstone arches in the world. Landscape Arch is the largest, with a span of 291 feet, but the most beautiful is probably Delicate Arch, viewed at sunrise or sunset, when the arch glows deep orange in its vast canyon setting.

South of Moab lies Canyonlands National Park, over 500 square miles of canyons, red rock pinnacles and great boulders which appear to be melting in the hot desert sun. Nearby Dead Horse Point State Park and the Needles District are popular destinations, but the wildest and most isolated part of the park is the Maze District, where six winding canyons composed of huge rounded rocks intertwine to baffle and humble even the most avid backpacker.

Capitol Reef National Park in south central Utah features the Waterpocket Fold, a 100-mile ridge of rock which has been eroded into narrow canyons and dotted with giant domes of white sandstone. The lush Fremont River cuts through the park, much of which is still remote and rugged wilderness. Zion National Park in the southwest corner of the state also contains such wilderness, on either side of colorful Zion Canyon and the Virgin River. The thrilling hike along the precipitous Angels Landing as well as the cooling waters of the well-hidden Emerald Pools and sheer cliffs of the Gateway to the Narrows makes Zion a hiker's dream come true.

But perhaps the highlight of a trip to southern Utah is the astounding Bryce Canyon National Park. The Paiute Indians called Bryce 'the place where red rocks stand like men in a bowl-shaped canyon.' The pink, orange and white pinnacles and spires, carved into this natural amphitheater by seasonal erosion, seem to change shape and color throughout the day as the sun moves across the sky. There is no better way to experience Bryce Canyon than to wander through it on foot and let the imagination run free.

National monuments of interest in Utah's canyon country include Natural Bridges, Cedar Breaks, Rainbow Bridge, Hovenweep and Dinosaur, on the Utah-Colorado border. There may well be no other state in the union which contains more fantastic natural wonders than Utah.

43 The delicate pink sandstone spires of Bryce Canyon National Park.

44/45 This panoramic view from Dead Horse Point State Park reveals Utah's characteristic landscape of high mesas, sheer cliffs and deep canyons.

46 A daring climber attempts the Supercrack, Canyonlands National Park.

47 The massive rounded boulders of the Maze District in Canyonlands make for challenging hiking.

48/49 Flaming orange in the setting sun, Delicate Arch stands on the brink of a canyon, with the white-capped La Sal Mountains in the distance, Arches National Park.

50 The Fremont River is an oasis in the dry slickrock country of south central Utah in Capitol Reef National Park.

51 Sheer canyon walls give way to cottonwoods and willows along the banks of the Virgin River at the Temple of Sinawava in Zion National Park.

52/53 An early morning view from Sunset Point in winter, Bryce Canyon National Park.

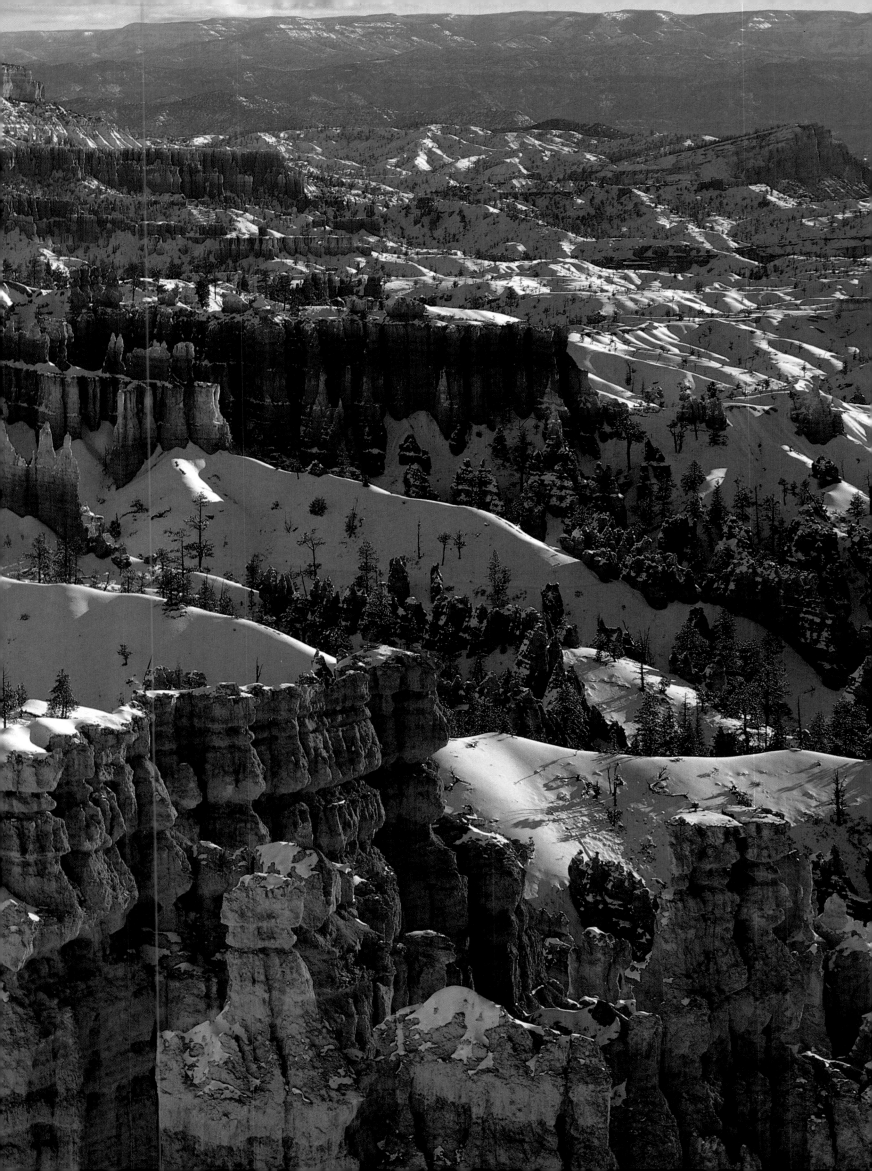

54 A blue sunset over the Great Salt Lake. Brigham Young brought the first Mormon settlement west to this isolated region in 1874.

55 The Mormon heritage is evident in Salt Lake City, capital of Utah. The modern highrise on the left is the headquarters of the Church of Latter-Day Saints, and to the right is the neo-Gothic Mormon Temple.

WYOMING, MONTANA AND IDAHO

The territory along the Continental Divide from South Pass, Wyoming all the way to the US-Canadian border in Montana includes some of the finest scenery in all of the Rockies. Jagged granite peaks rise dramatically above meadows colored with wildflowers in summer and covered by thick snow in winter, making for superb cross-country skiing. Here lives some of the most varied and interesting wildlife in North America: bighorn sheep, moose, elk, bison, and black and grizzly bear are only a few of the inhabitants of this great wilderness area.

At 13,804 feet, Gannett Peak in the Wind River Range is the highest point in Wyoming. The Winds rise sheer and steep above high, rounded valleys and glittering alpine lakes. Favorite spots include the beautiful Cirque of the Towers and Titcomb Valley. Just to the North lies the second highest peak in Wyoming, the Grand Teton (13,766 feet), center of popular Grand Teton National Park. The Teton chain rises abruptly for 7000 vertical feet from the sagebrush valley of Jackson Hole. Rafting on the Snake River and canoeing on the lakes at the base of the Tetons are good ways to experience the majesty of the mountains. For a real thrill the hike up amongst the great peaks themselves via steep Cascade Canyon to lovely Lake Solitude and back down through Indian Paintbrush Canyon, aflame with the orange spiky blooms in high summer, simply can't be beat.

In contrast, the topography of Yellowstone National Park, in the northwest corner of Wyoming, is very different indeed. Here the slopes are gentler and the forests and meadows uniform—ideal territory for wildlife. The park's most exclusive attraction, though, is the series of geyser basins which comprise the largest active thermal area in the world. Thousands of unpredictable geysers, hissing steam vents, brightly colored hot springs and pools, and percolating mud cauldrons recall an era long ago when the earth was in a constant state of flux. Old Faithful Geyser and the multicolored Mammoth Hot Springs are park favorites, as is the Grand Canyon of the Yellowstone, whose golden canyon walls give the park its name.

A land of sharp peaks and ridges, hanging valleys, turquoise lakes and numerous glaciers, Glacier National Park in northwestern Montana has more in common with the Canadian Rockies than with its southerly neighbors. In fact, in 1932 the Canadian Parliament and US Congress declared Glacier and Waterton Lakes, across the border in Canada, the first international peace park. Going-to-the-Sun Road in Glacier skirts picturesque Lake MacDonald before climbing steeply to Logan Pass, on the Continental Divide. Here one can imagine glaciers in the valleys on either side of the narrow Garden Wall steadily eating away at the pass before retreating many millions of years ago. The road then descends toward much-photographed St Mary Lake. In October, bald eagles provide a spectacle at Glacier as they gather to feed on spawning salmon. Towns of interest in western Montana include the ex-mining settlements of Bozeman and Virginia City.

Although not as visually striking as western Wyoming and Montana, central Idaho offers millions of acres of high altitude wilderness as well as some of the best whitewater rafting in the country. Hikers head for the volcanically formed Sawtooth Mountains, while rafters flock to Hells Canyon, the steepest, narrowest gorge in North America, or to the River of No Return, the wild Salmon River. The eerie landscape of Craters of the Moon National Monument is composed of dunes of volcanic black ash and smooth, hardened lava, a contrast to the green, heavily forested mountains which make up most of untamed central Idaho.

57 This breathtaking view from Artist Point of the Lower Falls in the Grand Canyon of the Yellowstone shows how Yellowstone National Park got its name.

58/59 Fiery Indian paintbrush and sweet-smelling purple lupine adorn a high country meadow below Warbonnet and Warrior I and II at Cirque of the Towers in the Wind River Range, Wyoming.

60/61 A gentle summer sunrise over beautiful St Mary Lake, Glacier National Park, Montana.

62 Daybreak over Horstmann Peak above Fishhook Creek Meadow in the Sawtooth Mountains, Idaho.

63 Rain clouds linger over a ranch in the Upper Coeur d'Alene River Valley, Idaho.

64/65 Clements Mountain rises behing Going-To-The-Sun Road at Logan Pass, Glacier National Park, Montana.

65 A favorite destination in Glacier is the Hanging Gardens near Logan Pass, known for its brilliant display of wildflowers.

66 top The majestic bald eagle can sometimes be seen high above the wild rivers of the Rockies.

66 bottom Black bears may look cuddly but are better viewed from a distance. Adults are five to six feet tall and weigh from 200 to 500 pounds.

67 top A bison is covered by frost after a snowstorm in Yellowstone's Hayden Valley.

67 bottom A bull moose grazes peacefully in the pristine wilderness.

68 The Green River Rendezvous in Pinedale, Wyoming commemorates the annual gathering of the Rocky Mountain fur trade. Present-day mountain men display their skills in various competitions.

69 Arches made of elk antlers stand at the entrance to the town square in Jackson, Wyoming. At the famous Million Dollar Cowboy Bar, saddles serve as barstools.

70/71 A cowboy ropes a calf at the rodeo in Cheyenne, Wyoming.

72/73 The Grand Tetons are enveloped in cloud as the Snake River catches the winter afternoon light at Grand Teton National Park, Wyoming.

74/75 The Minerva Terrace at Mammoth Hot Springs forms melting steps amidst the rolling hills of Yellowstone National Park, Wyoming.

76 Old Faithful's spectacular plume makes it the most famous geyser at Yellowstone.

76/77 Yellowstone's Midway Geyser Basin along the Firehole River is an active thermal area containing numerous geysers, fumaroles (steam vents) and hot springs.

CANADA

The Canadian Rockies, in Alberta and British Columbia, extended from Waterton Lakes National Park on the US-Canadian border to the virtually inaccessible wilderness north of Jasper National Park, on the British Columbia/Alberta border. Soaring, craggy peaks and deep, broad glacial valleys give this land a top-of-the-world feeling unsurpassed by the ranges to the South. Lakes colored dazzling blue by glacial melt, mountainsides cloaked in brilliant yellow by alpine larch in autumn and meadows blanketed with varicolored wildflowers in spring and summer are only a few of the scenic splendors offered by the Canadian Rockies. Plentiful wildlife as well as numerous recreational activities make this Canada's favorite vacationland.

Calgary, Alberta is the gateway to the Canadian Rockies. Nearby oil and gas exploration have allowed Calgary to benefit from the modern energy boom, and the natural attractions of the Rockies just to the West increase Calgary's appeal. Each summer the Calgary Stampede, the biggest rodeo and wild west show in North America, draws thousands of tourists to such events as the exciting chuckwagon race and traditional Indian dances which recall the rich history of the area.

The first national park established in Canada was Banff, and it remains, along with Jasper National Park to the North, the jewel of Canada's park system. Banff's hot springs drew well-heeled travelers at the turn of the century, and the Banff Springs Hotel and Chateau Lake Louise retain the feel of European spa resorts even today. Banff townsite lies in a remarkable location, with the Rockies rising broad and high on the West. Favorite scenic areas in the park include Lake Louise, Moraine Lake in the superb Valley of the Ten Peaks, Peyto Lake and Bow Summit. Fine views can be had from the base of Mounts Victoria and Lefroy, and for the hardy the hike up these peaks, as well as to the exquisite Egypt Lakes area and many other, more remote parts of the park, provides a mountain 'high' not likely to be forgotten.

The drive north along the Bow River soon joins with the Icefields Parkway, which runs for 143 miles through the center of the Canadian Rockies all the way to Jasper townsite and Jasper National Park. Canada's largest national park, 92 percent of Jasper's area is high country—mountains, alpine meadows and glaciers, the largest of which is the Columbia Icefield which covers a vast 125 square miles. Angel Glacier, on Mount Edith Cavell, is one of the most popular in the park as it is easy to reach. Maligne Lake and Athabasca Falls are other favorite park options. Perhaps the most beautiful area is the broad Tonquin Vally, which holds the gemlike Amethyst Lakes and is surrounded by the imposing peaks of The Ramparts. A breathtaking view of Jasper's wilderness can be had from the top of Whistlers Mountain, accessible by tramway or, always preferable, by foot.

Other national parks include Waterton Lakes, in Alberta, just across the border from Glacier National Park, Montana; Yoho, in British Columbia, appropriately named for the Cree word meaning 'wonderful!'; and Kootenay, in British Columbia, bounded by Yoho to the North, Banff to the East and Assiniboine Provincial Park to the Southeast. All of these feature the magnificent high country and variety of wildlife for which the Canadian Rockies is known and loved.

Provincial parks south of Jasper, smaller in area than the national parks but not lesser in grandeur, include Top of the World, Elk Lakes, Kananaskis, Mount Assiniboine, Hamber and Mount Robson (also the name of the highest peak in the Canadian Rockies, at 12,972 feet). North of Jasper, the Rockies begin to diminish in size and road access becomes limited and difficult. The southwest corner of the Willmore Wilderness, just north of Jasper, is the last outpost of the glacier-carved alpine country characteristic of the Rockies. The Continental Divide veers sharply to the West north of the Willmore, signalling the northern terminus of the great Rocky Mountain chain.

79 A hiker surveys the grandeur of the Canadian Rockies at Yoho National Park, British Columbia.

80/81 A fan of canoes decorates beautiful Lake Louise in Banff National Park, Alberta.

82 The peaks of the Canadian Rockies rise abruptly from the plains, as this view over Banff townsite shows.

83 Framed by a rainbow, Athabasca Falls thrills visitors to Jasper National Park, Alberta.

84 A traditionally clad Indian woman participates in the Calgary Stampede, the largest rodeo and wild west show in North America.

85 Calgary, Alberta, at night. Canada's oil capital is also the gateway to the Canadian Rockies.

86 The 36-hole Kananaskis Golf Course, west of Calgary, is splendidly set in a green valley beneath lofty peaks.

87 The Prince of Wales Hotel in Waterton Lakes National Park, Alberta. Waterton Lakes and adjoining Glacier National Park in Montana were declared the first international peace park in 1932.

88/89 Striking turquoise Moraine Lake occupies the Valley of the Ten Peaks in Banff National Park.

90/91 Robson Glacier and Mount Robson as seen from the slopes of Mumm Peak, British Columbia. At 12,972 feet, Mount Robson is the highest peak in the Canadian Rockies.

92 Egypt Lake in Banff National Park is a backpacker's paradise.

93 A cross-country skier and his husky enjoy a solitary outing in Jasper's exquisite Tonquin Vally.

94/95 Rocky Mountain bighorn rams at rest far above treeline in Jasper National Park.